NO Friends?

NO Friends?

The NO-SERIES *Presents*

NO Friends?

How to Make Friends Fast and Keep Them

No-To-Know Publication

ISBN 978-1-517-66577-7

Printed in the United States of America

First Edition

CONTENTS

99 - Your Friends Are My Friends AND My Friends Are Your Friends

NO Friends?

NO Friends?

Chapter 1

Why You Need Friends

The Desire To Belong

Companionship is more than a desire driven by loneliness; it is a basic human need!

We are social creatures, and we need to belong to some form of social order to feel complete.

Nothing says what this social order has to be; it can be centered on a religion, a political system, or a love of chocolate ice cream. The glue that holds the tribe together is not as important as the *existence of the tribe*.

This need for companionship is why humans crave contact with other humans. We need **friends,** and a lack of friendships will create feelings of sadness and loneliness.

Sure, a person can get used to a lonely existence, but it will never feel natural because it will always feel like something is missing.

Anyone would get lonely at the prospect of spending every day alone.

We can attempt to ignore it or numb it with drugs, but the sadness and loneliness will continue to haunt us.

The only way to satisfy nature, and prevent obscene credit card debt due to late night online shopping sprees inspired by boredom and depression of loneliness or stuff your face with extra snack-crave to find comfort in food with that belly-fat...is to **make and maintain friends.**

Be honest, do you really need an ice cream machine that polishes your shoes and waxes your car? *No.* No one does.

We All Want Friends

Of course, you probably already know that there are *no substitutes for friends.*

You feel it each time you start something new, like the first day at a new school or a new job. You instinctively know that you will need allies in a situation like this, so you will unconsciously begin to build a catalogue of people who could be potential allies.

This list often begins by the people that are helpful to you. You know the ones; they smile at you when you ask a question and patiently explain the process.

As **helpfulness** *inspires* **feelings of trust**, you will feel supported by them, and comfortable approaching them.

After you begin to feel that you can trust a person, it is easy to begin casual conversations.

If they are wearing a t-shirt of a band that you like, tell them you are also a fan. If it is located in an area of your body that won't get you in trouble for being flashing Tom, show off that regrettable baby ink you got for that band unexpectedly after you hardcore night of drinking too many beers at their last concert you attended. You can spend a few minutes sharing concert war stories or opinions of the band's latest album.

If they have pictures of kids on their desk, ask if the kids are theirs and be sure to comment on how adorable the little tykes are. Parents love talking about their kids, and are thrilled when others are interested in hearing how they had to pull a snake out of their son's jacket pocket when doing the laundry.

If you happen to have kids, you can use the snake in the pocket story as an opportunity to connect on a personal level by telling them how your son likes to play with the worms in your garden. This will give you both the opportunity to laugh at a gross story and share a boys-will-be-boys sigh.

Creating such **personal connection** will move you into a position of *being an equal* with the person you are attempting to connect with.

Now, you are not just a newbie that needs direction; you are also a fellow parent that can understand their struggles and share in their frustration and joy. It seems like a simple idea that can't have much impact, but you will see your interactions with the person change substantially. The smile that you receive from them will be more than a friendly gesture; it will become a **friendly hello** to someone they enjoy talking to.

When the person approaches you, they won't just ask about *how's work* or a *class is going*. Instead, they will ask about your dog.

The feeling of **intimacy** that is created can build a foundation for a *meaningful friendship*.

Nature's Way Of Telling You To Connect

Nature tells us that we need a **social order**, but what function does the social order serve?

It actually serves many functions, and all of them have helped to shape human evolution and sustain the population. Even at the earliest stages of human evolution, our survival depended on existence within a tribe.

Of course, some humans probably did try to survive on their own, however, what we know about human survival during that time would suggest that they wouldn't have survived outside of the tribe for long.

That feelings of loneliness you experience from a lack of friendship are a survival instinct. It is nature's way of telling you to make friends if you want to survive.

It is up to you to stop making excuses and listen to what nature is telling you.

Find Your Tribe

However, it can sometimes be difficult to find people that you can connect with.

You may enjoy activities that are not widely enjoyed by others around you. This situation can certainly make it difficult for you to find new friends, but you can improve this situation with a change in environment.

If you are not finding friends in your current hang-outs, consider some new places to socialize.

Don't think about what the hot new place is to make friends. Instead, concentrate on establishments and events that are centered on your interests. It doesn't matter if you don't know anyone because...you know that you share a common interest with everyone there, and that is the first crucial element of building the foundation for building meaningful friendships.

Your tribe is absolutely out there, the trick is finding them and making that critical connection. If you surround yourself with people that share your interests, you will find more success in creating connections that will lead to a meaningful friendship.

Whatever your interest, no matter how nerdy or uncommon it is perceived to be, there is a group for it.

Seriously, you can find anything on the Internet.

Even now you still survive from belonging to a tribe, although it may not feel like you are a part of one. There are many barriers between others and us in our tribe, and it can make us feel isolated and alone.

You probably feel like you provide yourself with food because you are the one who goes to the grocery store. After all, it is you that pushes the cart through the store and fill it, you check yourself out at a machine and then carry your groceries home yourself. You can do all of this without speaking to another human being, even though they surround you.

However, the food didn't instantly appear at the grocery store.

Others in your tribe grew the food, or raised the animals from which the products came. Others in your tribe packaged the food and brought it to the store. Still others in your tribe arranged the food in the store so you can easily acquire the food you need to sustain yourself.

You are able to eat because others in your tribe made it possible, and you would likely die without them.

Make Friends Or Cease To Exist

In our modern world, friendship is no longer necessary to eat because you are no longer required to interact with your tribe to acquire food.

However, friendship is still necessary for other important parts of human evolution, like **procreation.**

It seems silly with over seven-billion people on the planet to think that humans need to continue to procreate to survive, but if we stopped procreating the human race would die out when the current human infants reach the end of their life span. That would only give us about 80-years, which is a blink of an eye in terms of evolution.

The existence of humans beyond a few decades into the future demands that we continue to procreate, and that demands that friendships be formed.

Sure, procreation has been achieved by more than one set of humans who found that they despised each other later, but they were obviously able to set that aside for at least a few minutes to create a new life.

Procreation requires there *to be some kind of connection* between two people, even if that connection is temporary and fueled by cheap booze.

The benefits to the population extend far beyond procreation.

A social species tends to only need to produce fewer offspring because the offspring have a higher chance of reaching adulthood. This is due to the friendship of the adults, which provide *protection* and *nurturing*.

Turtles need to produce hundreds of offspring at a time to ensure that a few will make it to adulthood, as most will perish as juveniles. Those juveniles serve to further another species' survival by providing a source of food.

However, humans are at the top of the food chain. Our babies aren't meant to feed dingoes, but our offsprings still need a great deal of support and protection.

A Friend In Need

This need to be taken care of...also creates a need to take care of others. You not only need friends, others have a *need to be YOUR friend.*

Yes, they need your support, but it is more than that. They will feel a need to be your friend because everyone needs friends.

Having friends isn't only a basic need for you; it is a basic need for everyone. A life without friends is nor lonely for just you: it is lonely for everyone.

If you don't have much friends, or lack thereof, it is not productive to dwell in the negative emotions caused by a lack of friendship.

Friendship is how we satisfy our primal urge to belong to the tribe. You know, that tribe that you depend on for your survival.

Our emotions are meant to guide us into doing what is best for the survival of the human race.

This is why you feel lonely and left out when you are not part of the group, and everyone else does too.

Those **negative feelings** are nature pushing you into social interactions so that the human race can continue to thrive.

The only way to lose feelings of loneliness is to join the tribe.

Until you do, nature will let you find no peace.

Chapter 2

The Myth About Friendship

What Is A Friend

Do you know what a friend is? *Are you sure?*

The definition of **friendship** is a *state of mutual trust and support between allies*. It is a relationship that exists between people, companies and even countries.

However, did you notice that lack of the word *"like"* anywhere in that definition?

A person liking you...has nothing to do with them being friends with you.

Everyone has friends they wouldn't say *they like all that much*, and many people who are their friends, *vice versa*, don't like them all that much either.

You may not like them, but this isn't a popularity contest; it is a friendship, and it has nothing to do with **likability**.

Yet, others would consider these *"less likeable"* people as friends because people know they can trust them and count on their support.

Now that doesn't mean that you won't have friends that you like, because you will discover that several of your friends will be your favorite people on the planet, but that isn't the reason they are friend material; *trustworthiness* and *support* make them friends.

What Makes A Friend

You will also find yourself surrounded with people that you like, but wouldn't refer to as friends. Instead, they are an **acquaintance** or a *"person you know."*

They are the kind of people that are fun to be around, but you wouldn't trust them as far as you could throw a grand piano, so it serves you well to not let these people in too close, and the best way to do that is...to not confuse them as a friend.

When on a quest to make new friends, it is important to understand the difference between *"people you like"* and *"people that are your friends."* They are not always one and the same.

In fact, forget about likability, because that isn't at the **core** of a friendship that is in the **developmental** stages.

There are only <u>two questions</u> that need to be answered here:

Can you trust this person? And will this person support you?

If you answered *"yes"* to both of those questions, then you have a friend regardless of what you think of their personality. Plus, if you happen to like the friend that is merely an unexpected perk.

The Friendship Factor

Of course, you should also seek out people that you like. You can't surround yourself with personalities you find irritating and expect to be happy.

This is where those friends that you don't like can come in handy, as they can help you expand your circle of friends by including you in their clique. Their circle of friends likely contains many people that share the same values and ethics that encourage you to trust this ally.

Within this group, you will be able to find others that share the same qualities that inspire trust and support that are packaged into a more likable personality.

Once you adjust your view of friendship having to like somebody, you will find it is easier to make friends because you will no longer be overlooking people that you don't like all that much.

These people serve a purpose, and popular people know this. Popular people are often shunned for being shallow, and then envied for being rewarded with many friends.

Those that are confused about the true nature of friendship often fail to see that many friends are the reward of being shallow because friendship itself is shallow in the beginning.

In reality, people with many friends often dislike most of them, but they understand that friendship is not about liking each other. Liking each other is something else entirely.

Popular people have divorced the idea of liking people and being friends with them because it is a proven strategy that works time and again.

You are not going to be able to reinvent the wheel here, so stick with what works. It is important to understand that you shouldn't try to make everyone your best friend.

Make Many To Find The Few

There are many levels of friendship, and the **BFF types** are an elite class of friends. Think of BFFs as *The Ballad Of The Green Berets*: "One hundred men will test today, but only three win the Green Beret."

Becoming best friends is a long road, and it takes time to develop that kind of friendship, so don't expect much in the beginning. The BFF stage will come later.

Don't let yourself become bitter because the popular people understand the nature of friendship better than you do. Instead, learn the true nature of friendship.

You will naturally come across people you like along the way, but don't exclude someone just because you don't like him or her all that much.

If you hate the person, *fine*, you hate the person, but this is more about relaxing your standards than abandoning them entirely.

You are merely casting a wider net, not dredging the bottom of the waters.

Chapter 3

Why Some People Have Many Friends

The Friendship Value

Have you ever noticed that some people never seem to lack for friendship?

They appear to have a magnetic personality that causes people to be drawn to them.

Want to know the truth?

It has nothing to do with their personality; it has everything to do with their ability to add value to the lives of the people around them.

They place themselves squarely in the center of many universes, and people who understand the true nature of friendship can't resist gravitating toward them.

They find themselves pulled into the orbit of these magnetic people because people with many friends put out a vibe of being trustworthy and supportive.

After all, they must be trustworthy and supportive to have acquired so many friends.

You see this kind of joke made often on television and in movies:

Two friends, **Friend A** and **Friend B,** will be at lunch. Some jerk walks up to the table because he is *a friend* of **Friend A.** The jerk will say something stupid or obnoxious, which will *embarrass* **Friend A** and *offend* **Friend B.** At this point, the jerk will then walk away, completely unaware of how awful he was. This is the point at which **Friend B** will ask **Friend A,** *"Why are you friends with that guy?"* **Friend A** will respond by shrugging and saying, *"He gets me a deal on my oil changes."*

We are taught to believe that this is the wrong frame to be at for a friendship, and it certainly is not the foundation for a meaningful relationship; that is why it is set up as a joke.

The Role Of Different Friends

There are many different kinds of friends that serve many different functions.

For example, you might have friends at work that you do not want to socialize with outside of the office because that is not the purpose that particular friendship serves. A coworker is able to empathize with the stress and pressure at work better than a friend or family member; and this is the sole purpose of the friendship.

It doesn't mean that it isn't a fulfilling friendship; it just means that despite the casual nature of the friendship, it is enough to satisfy both of your needs.

Remember that friendship is about **survival.**

Think of it as the scene of a survival show. Have you ever seen a survival show that is set on a utopic stage of clouds and rainbows?

Of course you haven't. Nobody would watch it. When people are watching a survival show, they want to see a half-starved human with frost-bitten toes fight a bear using a stick.

Now that is **survival of the fittest.**

Sometimes, it feels like it would be easier to face an angry grizzly bear than it would be to face a crowded room, but as you become more comfortable in social situations you will welcome the crowded room.

Higher Expansion. Lower Expectation

You have probably been told that when it comes to friendship, **quality** is more important than **quantity,** but popular people know that the number of friends matter; they realize that the value of friendship is not always weighed in warm and fuzzy feelings.

Are they shallow?

Absolutely, but that doesn't mean they won't make a good friend. After all, knowing them will expand your social circle.

Yes, that person may never be your best friend, but that doesn't mean that they won't add value to your life.

Are they the kind of people that you invite to your birthday party for the present?

Sure, but as long as you aren't rude to them, and you give them a pleasant environment to socialize in, why should they care? It's only a birthday party anyway. It isn't like you are asking them to be a Godparent to your child.

Without a doubt, thinking of a friend as someone that you like and care deeply about is a sweet thought, but, *realistically*, that comes later.

Remember, if you think of friends as only being people you like, you are slamming doors on opportunities to meet new people.

You have to think of each person you meet as an opportunity to make more connections, and thereby more friends, regardless of how likeable you find them to be initially.

You are going to have to give people a chance before they will give you one, and really it is only fair. They don't owe you anything; they don't even know you yet.

Give them a chance to get to know you, without putting pressure on them to always be at their best.

Everyone has a dark side to their personality, and everyone has bad nights that will bring that dark side out, so give people a break the first few times you meet them.

If they are consistently a jerk, then break ties with them guilt-free, knowing that you have done your due diligence. However, you might be surprised to learn that they weren't as bad as you first thought.

Chapter 4

How to Make Friends

The Biggest Mindset Shift

You know what a friend is, and you know why you need them...*now how do you find them?*

First you need to change the way you view the people around you. You can see them as **strangers** or you can see them as **potential friends**. This is an important distinction.

If you see people as strangers, they will be difficult to approach. Obviously, it can be intimidating to interact with a stranger.

However, by viewing the people that surround you as potential friends, it will make your life far easier to add that person to your high rolodex list of contacts.

Seeing people around you as strangers puts a barrier between you and them. On the other hand, accepting the people around you as potential friends creates paths for dialogue and connections.

Utilize Your Everyday Opportunities

There are many chance encounters throughout your day you can use to meet people

It sounds a bit old-fashioned to just walk up and introduce yourself to a complete stranger, but when done with confidence this is a fantastic way to go.

So the next time you are in the elevator traveling to work, try on a friendly smile for size and a polite hello to the person next to you. If they respond positively, make small talk. It is okay if the talk is generic at this point, and you can start with something as mundane as the weather.

It can be as simple as...

You: *"Whew! It is hot today."*

Them: *"No kidding! The air conditioning is broken in our office. It is miserable up there."*

You: *"Yikes! I hope they get it fixed quickly."*

Them: *"Me too."*

Your first encounter with the person may not be more than three sentences, but the next time they see you they will remember your pleasant encounter and give you an opportunity for another.

The next time you see them, you can continue the conversation:

You: *"Did they get the air conditioning fixed in your office?"*

Them: *"Yes, thank goodness, but now I need a coffee to wake me up because the heat made me so tired."*

You: *"I'm heading that way myself. I have a nine-month-old son, so I pretty much haven't slept in 9 months. I survive on coffee anymore."*

Them: *"When my son was nine-months, I thought I would never sleep for eight solid hours again. I also survived on caffeine."*

You: *"How old is your son now?"*

The conversation naturally takes off from there.

After some time, you will find that you have dozens of people saying good morning to you as you make your way to work. They will ask you about your children or a recent vacation.

It should all be very casual, but eventually you will find yourself getting coffee together and taking walks together during breaks.

These activities create the opportunity for connections, which is how bonds between people are created. It is a process, but once you understand the process it becomes much easier.

Meet Friends Online

Our modern world has placed many barriers between you and others in your tribe, and now you need to make those barriers work for you.

In order to do this effectively, stop thinking of those barriers as an obstacle.

You can use the technology that separates you from others in your tribe as a means of connecting.

The Internet is the single greatest invention of our time. Not only does it provide us with unlimited access to information, it also connects us to people around the globe.

When you think about it, the Internet has done more to create a global community than any other technological advance of our time. The Internet seems infinite, and in a way it is, but there are still corners of the Internet that you can join and not feel lost in the expansiveness of it all.

There are many websites devoted to making connections between people.

One of the best sites for this is **Meetup.com**.

Meetup.com provides people a place where you can connect with groups of people that you share interests with. The groups are created by people like you that want to engage a group of people in a particular area of interest. The area of interest could be knitting, reading or making the perfect martini.

Find a group, or create a group of your own, that is built around an activity you are interested on.

Meet Friends Offline

Join groups in your area so the events will be easy for you to attend.

Many people will experience anxiety at the thought of attending an event that is full of strangers, but the easier it is to attend the event, the more difficult it will be for your nerves to create good excuses to NOT attend.

It is easy to click the *"join"* button on a website, and then not go any further with it. You won't make any friends that way.

Get excited for the event by purchasing a new sweater or get your hair done. You will feel more confident if you look your best. This may seem silly, but people want to be around others that are fun and attractive, so be fun and attractive.

If you are nervous about engaging in conversation, take some time to consider what the event is focused around, and think about the topics that might come up in conversation. You don't need to know everything. Just enough to be able to carry your side of the conversation, and be able to ask interesting questions based on a foundation of knowledge.

Them: *"My new puppy chewed up another pair of shoes yesterday. Pretty soon I'm going to be forced to walk around in bare feet."*

You: *"When I got my dog, we used this spray called bitter apple. Dogs find the taste of it repulsive. You just spray it on whatever your dog is chewing on, and they will hate the taste so much they will give up trying to chew on it. I sprayed all of my shoes and lined them up against the wall. Then I watched my puppy try to chew on the shoes. He grabbed a hold of the first shoe, and immediately spit it out. So he moved onto the next shoe, and immediately spit that one out too. He did that to eight shoes before he finally gave up. It was fun to watch, and he hasn't tried to chew on a shoe since. Now we are trying to find a way to break him of begging. Have you come across anything that helps with that?"*

Them: *"It used to be that we never ate a meal alone in our house. Then we read a blog that suggested we never feed our dog from our plate. It was hard right away, but we were finally able to train ourselves to stop giving our puppy bites of food from our plate. Now he shows no interest in us when we are eating."*

You: *"Thanks! I'm going to give that a try."*

Prepare To Engage

Considering what conversations might occur will make it easier to engage in conversations going on around you.

You will have enough knowledge to contribute intelligently to the conversation, but still be able to learn from others and give them a chance to entertain you.

The act of **listening** to others speak isn't just polite, it is how you learn about them.

A person's personality will come out in conversation.

You will see it in the opinions they express, the expressions they use and their body language during the conversation.

These subtle hints will provide give you insight into the kind of person they are at the core, and help you decide if this person is someone you would want as a friend.

The Friendship Development Process

Developing friends is a process, and it requires effort on your part.

If friends were just going to fall into your lap, it would have happened already; hence, you need to take the initiative here.

It all begins with starting the initial **conversation**. This is usually the most nerve-wracking part, but in the next chapter we will discuss exactly how you can do this successfully.

After you have started the conversation, you will need to build a **connection**. If there is no connection, there will be no friendship. You can't expect the other person to do this alone. You will have to hold up your end too.

And once the connection has been made, you will have to **maintain the friendship** by being supportive and trustworthy.

Successfully starting the conversation, building strong connections, and maintaining a strong relationship will guarantee you will make, and keep, many wonderful friends.

Chapter 5

Starting the Conversation

Be The Initiator

Don't wait for someone to approach you; take the initiative and begin the conversation. It isn't a big deal, so don't let yourself get tense over it.

Also you don't want to be so relaxed that it appears you have recently swallowed a large handful of valium, but you don't want to be the guy with the twitchy eyes either.

Don't worry about being cool. Not because everyone is special, and *being yourself* is the only way to remain true to yourself, but because everyone has their own brand of **weirdness**.

If a person thinks you are weird, what they are really saying is *"I don't understand you and I don't want to try."*

People who are interested in trying to understand you will refer to you as **"delightfully quirky."**

The Best Way To Approach

A good place to approach people is anywhere **refreshments** are located. It is a great way to stumble into a conversation. Random conversations have a habit of spontaneously beginning where refreshments are located.

Don't think of it as walking up to talk to someone. Think of it as walking up to get a beverage. Smile thoughtfully and politely acknowledge those around you. Before you know it, *"Hey, do you know if they have Heineken at this party?"* will easily transition to *"So you are the youngest of 12 kids? Wow, what is that like?"*

You don't need to be the most charming person in the room in order to impress someone so don't set the bar that high.

It's kind of like the old joke about the friends that have a chance encounter with a bear while camping. The friends begin running away from the bear. One friend says to the other *"Are you crazy? You can't outrun a bear"* and the other replies, *"I don't have to outrun the bear. I just have to outrun you."*

If you think you need to be the most charming person in the room, it is easy to feel substantial pressure and develop those unwanted twitchy eyes.

Don't Have To Do All The Work

Most people enjoy talking about themselves...**so let them talk.**

When someone is trying too hard, people can often pick up on it; so don't try to win any Academy Awards here.

Show a **genuine interest** in what they are saying. You can demonstrate your genuine interest by *asking a question* here and there.

Questions do more than just show your interest in what the person is saying. Questions will also tell you a lot about the person, giving you greater insight into the chances of friendship with the person.

Them: *"I just started a new job this week, and it has been stressful."*

You: *"New jobs can be so stressful. What is your new job?"*

Them: *"I just began a management role in a start-up that develops mobile applications."*

You: *"Start-ups can be crazy, and management roles are always a lot of stress. What kind of apps does your company develop?"*

Them: *"Games mostly, but we also do some mobile apps for various websites."*

What NOT To Do

Skip the deep and meaningful gaze altogether. It often puts out a creepy stalker vibe. You want to sound like an interesting new friend that they are considering having coffee with, not creepy dude at the party they are considering taking out a restraining order against.

- Ask them about things you are genuinely curious about based on something they just told you.

- Don't ask about something you don't care about. If you find it boring, odds are they do too.

- And don't be that guy who asks something overtly personal; after all, you did just meet.

In the beginning, you might feel some anxiety, especially if you have been a devoted wallflower. As you grow more comfortable starting conversations, the anxiety will lessen.

However, at this initial stage, it is easy to let nerves get the best of you, which can lead to you saying something you will regret.

Don't use large amounts of alcohol to make you more social, as it only increases the risk of you saying something stupid. You don't want to be the guy that is wearing the lampshade on his head.

The trick is to take a moment to think about what you are saying. You have a short window of time to work with, as you need to respond within a second or two to keep up with the conversation. Otherwise, it looks like you weren't paying attention to what the person was saying, but you can take at least a second to arrange your thoughts before speaking and others will consider you thoughtful and deliberate.

The Art Of Mindfulness

A good way to practice arranging your thoughts is through the practice of **mindfulness.**

Mindfulness is the art of being aware of your thoughts and actions without passing judgment. The ability to remain in control of your thoughts and emotions can go a long way in preventing a faux pas.

If you can be aware without judgment, you will be able to self-correct.

This awareness will dramatically reduce your anxiety, giving you a relaxed and confident aura that will attract people. Just knowing you can self-correct will prevent most problems, since most of the time a conversational faux pas is rooted in nervousness.

Mindfulness will help you to feel in control of yourself, and the conversation. The feeling of control that comes from mindfulness will prevent those butterflies from ever forming in your stomach.

If you aren't nervous to begin with, you can't make a nervous mistake. Think of it as an insurance policy against putting your foot in your mouth.

Practice Mindfulness

A good way to begin the practice of mindfulness is to sit in a comfortable chair. Make sure you are completely comfortable.

Sometimes you will be instructed to close your eyes, but keeping them open is recommended because it will help you transition your thought processes to conscious moments.

You need to be able to control your thoughts and emotions when you looking people in the eye, not when you are sitting in a dark room with your eyes closed.

If you find you are having trouble concentrating, try closing your eyes in the beginning. However, once you are comfortable with your eyes closed, transition into practicing with your eyes open.

You can have the lights turned up or down, light a candle, or whatever makes you comfortable.

There are no hard and fast rules on what to wear or anything like that. Just arrange yourself and your environment to provide you with a comfortable atmosphere.

Once you are able to do this in a quiet space with your eyes open, practice with the stereo or television on.

After all, a social setting will not be you alone in a quiet space. Social settings are full of noise from people talking and music playing in the background.

Now let your mind wander. Acknowledge each thought that crosses your mind without judgment. It isn't good or bad. It is just a thought. You are not analyzing the thought; you are merely acknowledging the thought for what it is.

This takes some practice because humans are trained to evaluate everything in categories of good and bad. Just keep practicing, and you will find you are able to step back from the emotional process and focus on the logical process.

If you are having trouble concentrating, you might need a change of environment.

Instead of sitting in a chair, try lying down or walking. If you are practicing indoors, find a quiet space to practice outdoors. Turn the TV or stereo on, or off. Make changes to your environment as needed, until you find the perfect environment for you to be able to practice in.

Record Past Patterns

Some people keep a journal of their thoughts because it can reveal surprising patterns in the way that you think and approach people and situations.

As you become more comfortable, you should keep a journal also. You can also include a section in your journal for encounters with new people.

Record how you felt during the encounter and how you feel the encounter went.

Was it positive? Did you say something you wish you hadn't?

If so, what did you say, and why did you say it?

A journal can provide wonderful direction on your journey to make new friends. You can then review your encounters to see what works and what doesn't.

Create Necessary Niceness Small Talk

Practice making small talk with people that absolutely MUST be **polite**, like the cashier at the grocery store.

Cashiers have a boring job, and conversation is the one thing they have available to them that helps pass them pass the time. They are a wonderful resource for practicing conversation because they really are professional conversationalists.

Keep it casual; this is a cashier, not your shrink. You don't want it to get too personal.

Start with something casual and see where the conversation goes. Likely conversations will resemble something like:

You: *"How is your day?"*

Them: *"It is good."*

You: *"That's good to hear. Wow, I love that ring you are wearing."*

Them: *"Thank you so much. My grandmother gave it to me. It was her mother's wedding ring."*

You: *"That is incredible."*

Asking *how a person is doing* is a great generic way to begin a conversation because is shows the person that you are interested in what they are saying, but it won't sustain a conversation.

You might get lucky, and the cashier will share something in their answer for how they are doing that you can build on, but you will need to have something else in mind to continue the conversation in case they don't provide you anything to work with.

Take a moment to find a follow up comment that you can use to continue the conversation while they are telling you how they are.

A **compliment** is a great way to follow up. Compliment something they are wearing or their hair. Flattery will get you everywhere with people, so don't be afraid to use just a little bit of it.

Becoming A Great Conversationalist

All of these things together, along with your sparkling personality, will help you to create a memorable and positive first impression.

You may want to consider keeping some time open for coffee, which is perfect.

Conversational skills are one of those *"practice makes perfect"* kinds of things, and a coffee shop is a wonderful atmosphere to practice in.

Now that you have some ideas on how to start a conversation, you are well on your way to making some new friends.

Starting the conversation is often the most difficult part of making new friends.

Remember that you are not expecting much from people yet. You are just creating opportunities.

You have created the connection, but now you need to build the connection, which will get into next.

Exercise Assignment: Improving Your Conversation Skills

For the next seven days, make an attempt to turn every encounter with a cashier, waitress, barista, or other stranger that absolutely must be nice to you into small talk.

Stay away from alcohol during this exercise, as remaining sober during the practice stages will increase your chances for success.

Besides, many bartenders will admit that they only feel obligated to remain polite if they like you or you tip well.

With each interaction, ask them how they are doing, compliment them and thank them. It doesn't have to be fancy, and will likely go something like this:

You: *"How are you?"*

Them: *"Fine. Thank you."*

You: *"I love your hat."*

Them: *"Thanks! It's my favorite."*

You will go through the whole credit or debit script here while you pay.

You: *"Thanks. Have a good night."*

Them: *"Thanks. You too."*

With any luck, you will encounter several chatty people that are compelled to be polite under any and all reasonable circumstances. However, it is fine if the conversation isn't more than half a dozen sentences.

People have bad days, and six sentences may be all the other person can pull together.

Don't take it personally; it is a bit arrogant to assume that this person who doesn't know you at all would be so affected by your mere presence. Shake it off and remember that you have bad days too.

After seven days, you will find you have made small talk a habit.

The longer you continue to practice making conversation with strangers, the more comfortable you will be making conversation under any circumstances.

This exercise will not only teach you the art of beginning conversations by perfecting your small talk skills, it will also improve your overall conversation skills because you will be more relaxed when carrying on a conversation with someone that you don't know well.

<u>Chapter 6</u>

Building the Connection

After The Initial Conversation

You will find that it is easy to strike up a casual conversation with almost anyone in the right situation...but what about *after* that first conversation?

How many times have you met someone that you felt an instant connection with, you get along so well and have so much in common that it seems impossible that you won't become fast friends, and then you never hear from them?

So you call them and try to make plans, but they don't even remember whom you are. The situation becomes awkward for both of you, and so you both abandon the idea of becoming friends.

The best way to avoid the awkward situation just described is to make plans immediately!

Connect Immediately

Find a common interest, and then mention an event that is happening and ask if they are going.

If they show enthusiasm, offer to meet them there or pick them up and give them a ride. Don't just mention this in passing; make it a central part of the conversation so it will be impossible for them to forget.

And make sure that the event is not too far off into the future. You want to make plans for within the next few days to make sure that it will stay fresh in their minds.

Be sure to share your contact information, like phone numbers, so you can call or drop them a text the day before to confirm your plans or easily find them if you are meeting them someplace.

Asking for contact information can be awkward, and is a tricky road to traverse. Sometimes people are hesitant to give their phone number to someone they don't know.

Fear not! Social media is a fantastic option for staying in touch with people, and for many people it is less invasive than sharing their phone number.

Create fantastic Twitter and Facebook pages, and fill them with interesting posts. You are selling yourself on these sites, so give out positive vibes. Posts should be about you and how fun you are to be around. Some good examples are:

"Going to the Interpol concert tonight! Anyone else going to be there?"

"Just brought home a brand new 55" TV! I am thinking movie night next Saturday. Who wants to watch things blow up on a big screen??"

"Work sucked, but now that is done and I am heading to The Garage for a beer. Anyone else need to shake off a bad day? Come belly up to the bar with me."

Keep your posts fun and inviting. People don't want to come and hang out with someone that is going to bring them down. Save that for your close friends. When making new friends, keep it upbeat.

Put Effort In Building Connection

Remember that friendship is shallow in the beginning, and appearance will matter. Sure, it isn't a romantic date, but it is still a date nonetheless.

If you don't treat the occasion as being important enough for you put effort into your appearance, why would the other person feel like you want to be their friend?

Your appearance is an indication to others as to how important an event is to you. Obviously, this isn't a wedding, so you can put the formal wear away, but don't pull out the sweatpants either. Odds are you will be meeting a new friend for a casual affair like coffee, or maybe a movie.

Once again, use that wonderful resource we call the Internet to provide you with some direction on what colors and styles are considered hip this month.

Put together an outfit that is casual, and reflects your style, but don't try to wear something that is outside of your comfort zone for the sake of being trendy. You will only feel uncomfortable, and that just sends out a bad vibe.

We often condemn vanity, and judge people on their appearance all in the same breath. Don't feel guilty for caring about your appearance; be a little vain, and put your best self forward each and every time.

Give this new friend every indication that their friendship is valuable to you.

In addition to being pleasing in appearance, you will also have to be pleasing company. You will need to be interesting to listen to, and interested in what the other person has to say.

Remember that conversation is an exchange of information. You give some information, and you receive some information. This is how a successful conversation works.

So think of questions you can ask them. Like:

"I grew up in South Dakota. It was pretty quiet. What was it like to grow up in the city?"

"I heard you took a trip to Japan. I went a couple of years ago and really enjoyed myself. I was really blown away by some of the ceremonies. What did you think of the culture?"

"You just got a dog? I love dogs! I have a cocker spaniel at home named Gilligan. He is my little buddy. Maybe we can take them to the dog park together. What kind of dog did you get?"

Find Common Ground

Exchanging information is crucial to building the connection.

The information shared in conversation is how you find common ground. It is common ground that gives you a foundation to build the connection. The more you have in common, the more engaged the other person feels.

Common ground is how the connection between the two of you will grow.

Keep the event casual. If it is a big event, it can become a stressful event. You can't make the first attempt at spending time together painful.

If you do, they won't want to hang out with you again.

People want to do things that are easy, so make it easy. Otherwise, the next time you want to go out with them you might find they are busy *(translation, busy avoiding the hassle of going out with you)*.

Social events should be fun to attend. If they become work, it will turn people off from wanting to hang out with you.

Go to coffee. Spend an afternoon at the beach. Get lunch at a casual and quiet diner that is your favorite haunt.

It gives the other person a glimpse into your life, and what they could expect to be part of if they became your friend. It is also an easy event that will be easy to attend.

If every part of it is easy and pleasurable, a second *"friend date"* is pretty much guaranteed.

When you have established a friendship, you can make plans months in advance.

Maybe your favorite band will be coming to town or you want to take a weekend vacation together, but this is not an established friendship; so keep it simple, and in the near future.

Once as an established friend, you can make plans far in advance because you will have many opportunities to hang out and discuss the event beforehand.

If you try to do that with someone you don't know well, they will likely forget...*well, you can't blame them.*

You also want to make the first few follow up hangouts short and sweet events. You are taking each other out for test drives at this stage so don't push things.

Virtual Connection

Another handy aspect to technology and the Internet is social media.

Practically everyone is on Facebook or Twitter. It is a fantastic way to stay connected to people with minimal effort.

Find out what they use and connect to them on their favorite social media platform.

Most people consider connecting via social media an extremely casual event and are likely to accept the connection without thinking about it. You can learn a lot about them by the posts they make and share, and it gives you a chance to comment on the things they post.

Social media can really help to build a connection while keeping a safe distance.

Understand though that sometimes text doesn't come off right, especially if the person doesn't know you well.

Remember that in your online communications, and take care to edit carefully.

Don't try to pull of sarcasm with someone you don't know well. You are risking it not coming off well and being poorly received. You can try to explain yourself, but it often comes off as defensive. Don't lie about what you are thinking, but remember that text can come off as more aggressive than you intended.

Play Host/Hostess

Once you have a few connections, it is time to host a get-together.

Don't serve dinner, unless you are planning to order pizza. Dinner parties are a lot of work, and even the most seasoned host will have parties that flop.

Don't risk getting too fancy. Keep it simple, with minimal opportunities for something to go wrong.

Invite three or four people over for a late coffee date on a Saturday morning. It is Saturday morning, so keep it casual.

Make up a pot of your favorite brew and buy some tasty pastries to nibble on from your favorite bakery.

Seat and serve everyone in a comfortable area like a kitchen table with comfortable chairs or a living room, if you don't mind people drinking coffee and eating on your sofa.

If it is Saturday night, invite everyone over for a few drinks. Invite five or six people over, and serve snacks. Think bar snacks like pretzels and peanuts. You could even order a pizza.

This scenario also works well for movie nights or watching you favorite TV show with other fans.

Create an event that will be engaging to everyone you want to invite. Don't invite someone over for TV night to watch a show you know they don't like. Invite them for coffee instead, and save TV night for people that love "Breaking Bad" as much as you do.

Build It Or Lose It

Build the connection by being fun and easy to hang out with.

During this stage, this will be one of the most crucial aspects to your success. Don't be that guy that is difficult to hang out with. Clearly define the plans. If you keep people guessing, they will get tired of playing and stop hanging out with you.

Set firm plans, and keep to them. Don't be late. Don't cancel unless you absolutely must. And give your new friend your full attention during your time together.

Show that you are having fun and enjoying their company by laughing and keeping a cheerful attitude. Take the initiative by hosting some small events, and get on social media. Take advantage of the entire Internet and all it has to offer.

Building the connection is a *continual process*. It never ends. There is never a point where you have enough information about your very best friend.

The whole point of a meaningful friendship is that you will continue to share your lives and build on your connection for the entirety of the friendship. This requires an investment on your part, and theirs, in order to build that meaningful friendship.

Building the connection is an important step in building a new friendship, but now that you have built the connection you will need to **maintain the friendship**. Your new friend will have the right to expect certain things from you in order to maintain your status as a trustworthy and supportive friend.

Now it is up to you to do your part to maintain the friendship coming up next.

Exercise Assignment: Reach Out And Touch Someone

Scroll through the contact list in your phone and on your social media, making a list of people you could hang out with for at least one hour.

Think of activities they would enjoy, and reach out. You can call, text, email or post on their social media to deliver an invitation to hang out.

If someone is busy, just take a rain check and move onto the next person. Try a different person every few days until you find someone that is available.

Make solid plans for a casual event like lunch, coffee or a walk or run along a local trail.

The day after you hang out, send them a message telling them you had a good time. Suggest hanging out again sometime, and offer to engage in an activity that they expressed interest in.

It's okay to leave this open-ended. You don't want to come off as pushy. Let them suggest a time that would be convenient to get together again.

Make it a practice to reach out and initiate plans with someone, and schedule activities at least once every couple of weeks.

After some time, you will find people reaching out and making plans with you. Hanging out with friends will become a regular event.

Chapter 7

Maintaining the Relationship

It's Never Over

As the friendship continues, it will require **maintenance**. This means that you will need to spend time together developing fond memories so the relationship brings up positive feelings.

You will need to be there when the other person needs someone to lean on. This might mean 3 a.m. phone calls, so be the person who answers the phone. The other person will need to be able to count on you, and this constitutes inconvenience on you with rides to the airport and other unpleasant errands.

The upside is that you will be able to expect the same favors from them *(but don't push your luck)*. :)

In order to keep these favors coming, not only will you have to continue to provide your new friend favors, but also you will need to invest time into the relationship.

Just because it isn't a romantic relationship doesn't mean that it won't require your time and effort.

Hang Out Regularly

Short weekly activities are wonderful ways to keep in touch and continue to build your connection to your friend while also maintaining the friendship.

Some common <u>weekly activities</u> are:

- **Walking** - A weekly walking date is a fantastic opportunity to connect. This is time you can spend talking and strengthening your bond.

- **TV Show** - Maybe you both love the same television show. You can make plans to watch it together. Offer to host, and order pizza to show your friend a good time.

- **Play Dates** - Play dates for parents often turn into a break for parents *(if you're actually one)*. You can sit on a park bench and pass the time engaged in a lovely conversation with another parent while your kids burn off energy on the playground.

- **Pool/Bowling Leagues** - If you like to bowl or shoot pool, almost every area has one of these leagues. You form a team, and your team plays against an opposing team once a week. You get a night out each week with your friends, and you get to meet new people too.

- **Karaoke** - If you love to put on a show, and your friends do too, suggest a weekly or monthly trip to the karaoke bar. Pour down a few doses of liquid courage, and then get on that stage and give them all you got!

The whole point of a weekly activity is to have fun with your friend on a regular basis.

It gives each of you something to look forward to during the week, and it will involve an activity you and your friends will enjoy. It is important to create bonding experiences during the course of a friendship, and you will need these experiences throughout the life of the friendship.

Find something you and your friends enjoy doing, and make it a weekly event.

Cleaning Up The Friend's List

Remember that any relationship is about *give* and *take*, and before you can take, you need to have something to give. However, if you find that you are doing all the giving and they are doing all of the taking, it is worth dumping them.

You don't want to be draining on them, but you don't want anyone who is draining you either. It just isn't worth the effort on your part.

Remember, a friend will add value to your life. If they can't at least get you a deal on your next oil change, dump them.

If they are fun to hang out with, use them to hang out with when you need a fun crowd, but don't let them get too close. They might introduce you to some new people that can lead to more friends for you, but don't bother if you aren't getting anything out of it.

You need to be selective, and be careful who you're friends are *(as they say)*.

People dump friends in different ways.

The most common way is the **passive aggressive approach**. This approach is when you just ignore someone. You don't answer their phone calls, texts, emails or social media posts.

When you run into them, you feign being sooooo busy, *"Yikes! I am so sorry. Did I miss a text from you? Gosh, I didn't even see it.*

Life has been crazy, and I just haven't been able to keep up with everything."

Eventually the friend you want to dump will get the hint and move on.

If you prefer a more **direct approach**, you can just tell them that you don't feel like you have much in common.

Keep in mind that both of these options likely come with some blowback, especially if you share a circle of friends. Sometimes it is easier to just take a step back, keep some distance between you and them, and perfect the art of being busy anytime they want to get together.

Smoothing The Rough Bumps In Friendships

Things won't always be a bed of roses. Any relationship experiences slumps and rough times. Friendship is no different.

There will be moments where you will be disappointed in each other. There will be moments where you will be angry at each other. Just be an adult about it.

If the emotions are still running high, give it a few days to calm down.

Go to your corners and think things through. Consider what it is you are actually upset about. Think about what your friend is upset about, and consider their point of view. How important is the disagreement? Are they right about any of it? Even if they are wrong, is it worth apologizing just to smooth things over?

Try to consider the feelings of everyone involved.

Once enough time has passed, try calling your friend up to discuss the rift with them.

If you did something wrong:
- Apologize.
- Listen to how they feel about it.

- Acknowledge their right to feel sad, disappointed or angry.
- Offer to make it right, and ask your friend what they need from you in order to do this.

If you were the one wronged:
- Clearly explain exactly what it was that upset you.
- Clearly explain why it upset you.
- Tell your friend how it made you feel.
- Let your friend explain why they made the mistake.
- Tell your friend how they can make it up to you.

Good communication is the key to any successful relationship, including friendship.

Communication is important when you are getting along to build connections, but it is **most important** for *when you are not getting along*. Communication is how you will resolve your differences.

Friends always encounter differences, so be prepared to deal with it like an adult.

This is where a shared circle of friends comes in handy, as they can help you understand what the other person is upset about. They can also assist in communicating your feelings to the other person.

When you are both ready, you can meet each other heart to heart. You can each express what is upsetting you, and what you would like to see done to resolve the issue.

Disagreements are an opportunity to work things out.

After you have, you will each have a deeper understanding of each other and will be closer from the experience of working things out together.

One day you will both laugh over the dumb arguments you have had over the years.

That's just part of friendship.

Exercise Assignment: No Peg, It's My Bowling Night

Find some kind of **group activity** that meets on a regular basis, but there is a catch. You have to choose a group that is filled with the word that strikes fear into the hearts of many an introvert: strangers.

Go to the neighborhood bowling alley and join a league. Go to your neighborhood library and ask the librarian for recommendations on book clubs. Buy a copy of <u>The Art of French Cooking</u>, locate and join a Julia Child's cooking class and learn to pronounce "bon appétit" in a perfect Julia Child's imitation.

Whatever turns you on; just make sure you have some kind of social activity that takes place at regular intervals.

It cannot be a random event each week or month that you engage in with random people. It must be a group event where the members of the group are relatively consistent.

The point of this exercise is to engage in the full process of friendship. You will begin by building on the two previous exercise assignments, with an additional assignment for maintaining the friendship.

The event that you choose must be an event where you don't know anyone. You will *start conversations* with strangers, have a regular opportunity to *build a connection*, and *maintain the connections* you make over a period of time.

Leagues provide a casual opportunity to gather with a regular group of people, while consistently providing opportunities to interact with a group that you may not know as well. Some of the people in the groups that make up the opposing team may contain people you do not know at all.

An activity that is structured like this, gives you the best variety of ways to practice several techniques repeatedly.

You will spend each week starting conversations with people you don't know or don't know well, as well as building connections and maintaining friendships with your teammates. Plus it has a fun blue-collar atmosphere.

Do you lack coordination? Are you dangerous with a sharp stick or a heavy object in your hands?

If so, forget about pool, darts and bowling. You know, safety first and all. Maybe a book club would be more your speed.

Let's face it, this world is full of not the sharpest tools in the shed.

Besides, more people should be encouraged to read. A book club is an intelligent activity that encourages the use of critical thinking skills, and it is perfect for bookworms.

If you find a good book club, you will be introduced to new authors and titles you might have otherwise overlooked. You might find your new favorite book, and you will be given a regular opportunity to engage in a conversation with a regular group of peers.

This is a fantastic environment to practice the full process of friendship.

- In the beginning, you will be starting conversations with strangers, opening up the possibility of them becoming friends.

- After a few meetings, you will then begin to build connections with the regular members of the group.

- As you continue to participate in the group, you will transition into a stage of maintaining friendships with the regular members.

Can you cook a meal without setting off the smoke alarm?

Maybe a cooking class would interest you. In a cooking class, not only to do get to engage in all three of the processes of friendship, you also get to practice a skill that will allow you to host an impressive dinner party.

Invite people you met and connected with during the class to an informal dinner party at your home.

With practice, you will be able to serve a gourmet meal to a small group of people.

Good food and a relaxed atmosphere will make your dinner parties a special social occasion for all of your guests, and have them waiting anxiously for their next invitation.

Chapter 8

Friendless No More

You Have Come A Long Way

When you started reading from the beginning, you probably felt like you lacked the skills necessary for making new friends.

However, you know now that there are many different kinds of friends, and you no longer expect everyone to be your best friend right away.

You know the difference between being friends with someone and liking someone, and you have gained some insight into the way popular people view friendship.

Being real here. The utopic ideas of friendship, too often the tragic penalty of having watched too many John Hughes movies, have been discarded, and now you know friendship is a shallow business in the beginning that takes time to develop into something meaningful.

This understanding will help keep you from expecting more than you should right away, and will prevent you from feeling needlessly discouraged and disappointed.

Real friendship takes times to develop.

Go Out Make New Friends

You are also armed with fresh skills that will help you on your journey to finding new friends.

You have learned of many new places to look for friends online and in the real world. If you don't already have a free account on Meetup.com, go create one now.

You can also search the web for other websites devoted to making connections between people searching for friends.

You can also join a bowling league, or some other league that hosts a weekly event.

Even if you do not have a team, these leagues will often keep a list of singles that are looking to form a team. Ask the league's leadership about helping you find or form a team. Most leagues are happy to help.

Is bowling trashy blue-collar fun? *You're darn right it is, break out the PBR!* ;)

If that isn't your scene, try to find a book club or another group that is built around a more dignified interest that you share.

Begin Conversation To Connection For Friendship

You have also learned some tips on improving your conversational skills, and have some directions for real world practice.

Humans surround you, and so do opportunities to practice small talk, so start talking. There is nothing to fear.

Who cares if you say something stupid to a random stranger? Odds are you are never going to see them again anyway. They are the perfect pawns to practice and get the mistakes out of the way.

Once you have established communication and made the initial attempt at connecting, you have learned how to build on that connection.

After all, meeting new people doesn't do you much good in making new friends if you never see them again. You have learned the art of planning a successful opportunity to hang out in a one-on-one situation, and in a group setting.

Most importantly, you have learned to take the initiative by creating groups and hosting events.

Finally, you have learned what it takes to maintain a friendship. It is work, but you now know what you must do to encourage successful friendships that will carry you through the years to come.

Understanding the art of communication, as well as anticipating that there will be rough patches, will go a long way in cultivating a meaningful friendship.

As you cultivate these friendships, you will find that you will easily make more friends along the way. Yet, every day will not be an episode of *"Friends,"* but you won't feel like the Unabomber anymore either.

Your Friends Are My Friends
AND
My Friends Are Your Friends

We often want to introduce our friends to each other, and this creates a snowball effect. As you make new friends, you will meet their friends. Then, as you become friends with those people, you will meet more new people. Before you know it, your circle of friends will be bigger than you ever thought possible.

With the technology we employ in our daily lives, it is not thinking too big to know that you could have a global network of friends. This will create new opportunities for networking and social activities that will be beneficial to your personal and professional life.

Stop spending your days in a lonely fog. Get out of the house and use the strategies illustrated throughout, and you will soon find that the loneliness has abated and your dance card is full.

You will feel like a new person, with more energy and creativity than you ever had before, all because you made some new friends.

New friends are such an invigorating experience. It reminds you that life is full of possibilities if you are willing to create opportunities and take advantage of the ones that fall at your feet.

Don't let those possibilities escape you! Make new friends now!

NO Friends?

PERSONAL THANK YOU!

We can't thank you enough for entrusting in us to help you improve your life with our <u>NO-To-KNOW Series</u>.

We hope this has helped you, and you have gotten a ton of value.

If you can leave us a review on where you have purchased this book, we will be extremely appreciative in helping us improve the series.

Be sure to check other books in the NO-To-KNOW Series.

If you have a topic you like for the series, be sure to let us know, as well as we always love your feedback.

Thank you!

- All of us here at NO-To-KNOW Publication

NO Friends?

Made in the USA
Las Vegas, NV
23 December 2021

39292591R00062